The
JUICE
2010-11

by
Matt Skinner

The Juice 2010 – 11
by Matt Skinner

The Juice Team
and Mitchell Beazley
would like to send
a big thank you to
all the wine merchants,
agents, retailers, and
producers who helped
with the research for
this book.

The price key
To be used as a guide only

$~$$$$~~~~~Under $10

$$~$$$~~~~~$10 – 20

$$$~$$~~~~~$21 – 30

$$$$~$~~~~~$31 – 100

$$$$$~~~~~Over $100

Disclaimer: Wherever possible, the
current release of each wine has
been selected in line with the vintage
availability supplied by the winery
and/or agent or importer. Vintage
and price information is correct as
far as possible, but demand can
affect which vintage is available and
pricing and availability can differ
from state to state and between
retailers. In wine entries, the website
of the winery, importers, or distributor
is shown. Please contact the listed
website for the most up-to-date
information on your chosen wine(s)
and retailers in your area.

First published in the U.S. and Canada in 2009
by Octopus Books USA,
c/o Hachette Book Group USA,
237 Park Avenue, New York, NY 10017
www.octopusbooksusa.com

An Hachette Company
www.hachettebookgroup.com

ISBN 978 1 84533 527 4

Library of Congress CIP data is available on request.

Set in Helvetica Neue LT and AG Book Stencil

Colour reproduction by United Graphics, Singapore
Printed and bound by Toppan, China

The author and publishers will be grateful for
any information that will assist them in keeping
future editions up to date. Although all reasonable
care has been taken in the preparation of this
book, neither the publishers nor the author
can accept any liability for any consequences
arising from the use thereof, or the information
contained therein.

Commissioning Editor Rebecca Spry
Editorial Director Tracey Smith
Managing Editor Hilary Lumsden
Senior Editor Leanne Bryan
Copy-editor Susanna Forbes
Proofreader Jo Richardson
Art Director Pene Parker
Concept Design Matt Utber
Layout Design Spencer Lawrence
Photographer Chris Terry
Production Manager Peter Hunt

Contents

It's a jungle out there

That's for sure. Unemployment is up. Spending is down. Times are tough. Non-essential buys have become a thing of the past, and there are many things we're prepared to go without, but thankfully history suggests that wine isn't one of them.

Welcome to the first US edition of *The Juice*. As a regular visitor to your country, it's an honor for me to be able to give you my spin on the world of wine. In this guide I've made a conscious effort to shine the light on producers big and small who are making great wine that you can get your hands on and, more importantly, great wine that you can afford. Some are well known with established reputations, while others are modern classics in the making.

And while digging up bargains has always been close to my heart, in this book I concentrate on wines that give more for less.

And then I got to thinking, how else can wine add value to your life? Here are a handful of suggestions that should help you endure the gloomy times that are upon us. To start with, dine consciously. How long is it since you shared a bottle of wine and a decent conversation over a homecooked meal? Shop locally. Independent wine stores need you now more than ever— get to know those in your area, take their advice, buy their wines, and help keep them trading. Bring your own. Find out which local restaurants have a BYO licence and support them. Buy a wine book. You'll watch less TV as a result, and you might even learn something! Open your mind. Often the best-value wines are those from lesser-known varieties and places. Start a wine group— the kind where everyone brings a bottle, you taste, talk, listen, and laugh. Visit a vineyard. Local producers need your support. And if you live within striking range of a wine region, make a day of it—or stay the weekend!

Keep smiling x

How it all works

What began life as a weekly email sent out to friends and workmates in a vain attempt to help them drink better has now become a regular distillation of my drinking year. *The Juice 2010–11* combines 100 wine recommendations together with a few handy tips and a little bit of wisdom. Think of it as the big kids' survival guide to "planet wine" or, better still, a huge step toward better drinking.

So here's the drill. I thought that rather than ranking the wines 1 to 100, it'd be far more useful if I grouped the wines by occasion, so I've split my 100 wines into four easy groups of 25 wines each: Skimp, Dine, Drink, and Splurge. Bearing in mind the tough times we're all in the middle of, I've been on the lookout even more for wines that over-deliver on value. And there's something here for everyone: every taste, every budget, and every occasion.

I've made every effort to ensure that both price and vintage are as accurate as possible at the time of publication (*see also* page 2). Each wine entry includes the website of the importer or distributor or winery —the idea being that you contact the company and find out the nearest stockist to you. I hope that you should be able get your hands on most of the following 100 wines without too much heartache.

Happy drinking!

Awards time always brings about a certain sense of dread. Right at the start, there is very deliberately no ranking system in *The Juice*, there are no star ratings, and no scores out of 100. Pedestals are not what this guide has ever been about. Irrespective of price, each of the wines featured in this book deserve to be here for one reason or another. That said, throughout the course of the year there are always one or two wines—and one or two names—that repeatedly crop up, and for that reason I think it's important you know what and who they are. So without apology, these are the wines that I talked about, enthused about, and repeatedly sniffed, swirled, and slurped this year.

Best wine

Castellare di Castellina Chianti Classico 2006
Tuscany, Italy

For many years Castellare have made, and continue to make, beautiful wine—simple as that. Located high up (1200 feet) in the postcard-like hills of Castellina in Chianti, this estate, owned by Paolo Panerai since 1979, bucks the trend for power and concentration, producing traditionally styled wines from its 82 acres (33 hectares) with breathtaking purity and great elegance.

From the warmth of the 2006 vintage, this is an incredibly pure snapshot of Sangiovese, where a nose of pure morello cherry, leather, and tobacco makes way for a plush, mineral-textured palate framed by trademark chalky Sangiovese tannins, fresh acidity, and a clean, drying finish. With hunting prohibited on the estate, Castellare also doubles as a natural wildlife refuge for many local animals—including the (annually changing) wild birds that feature on the front labels. A simply outstanding wine from an outstanding producer. (*See page 178.*)

THE JUICE AWARDS 2010-11

Best bargain

d'Arenberg
The Stump Jump 2007
McLaren Vale, Australia

Since 1943, d'Arry Osborne has firmly focused his attention on handcrafting some of the most high-quality examples of Grenache and Syrah produced anywhere in the New World. Armed with a traditional basket press, plenty of enthusiasm, and some of the oldest plantings (c.1890) of these varieties to be found outside of France's southern Rhône Valley, this estate is now regarded as one of the finest of its kind. That said, one of the most endearing qualities of d'Arenberg is that as consistently good as the wines are—and that's very good—they continue to remain consistently affordable.

The Stump Jump red, an all-terrain blend of unwooded bush vine Grenache (50 percent), Shiraz (29 percent), and Mourvèdre (21 percent), is a great example of exactly that. Like other wines in the d'Arenberg range, production includes fermentation in head-down, open-top fermenters followed by gentle basket-pressing. (*See* page 135.)

Best producer

Dr Loosen
Germany

With holdings throughout Germany's most famed vineyards together with ecologically sound and sustainable practices, Ernie Loosen is widely regarded as not only one of the finest exponents of Riesling anywhere but as one of the greatest white winemakers on the planet.

His most basic offering, Dr L Riesling, is an accessible and pretty wine that runs with all the precision of a finely tuned BMW, while his most sought-after wines from the super-steep, south-facing, free-draining, slate-ridden vineyards between Bernkastel and Kindel are the stuff of legend. And although there have been numerous joint ventures around the world, Loosen has always been a fierce champion of the German wine industry, of the integrity of its wines, of valuing quality over quantity, and for bending over backward to reintroduce quality German wine to the rest of the world. (*See* pages 106 and 114.)

Varieties, places, & styles

Wine comes in all different shapes and sizes: big wines, little wines, fat wines, skinny wines, good wines, great wines, and wines that will absolutely blow your mind. And while what happens in the winery can play a big role in determining how a wine might end up tasting, grape variety, place, and style will all have an impact too. With the number of varieties and styles now running well into four figures, here's a brief rundown of those that grace the pages of *The Juice*.

The Whites

Chablis
(sha-blee)

Chablis is the name of a town in the northernmost part of Burgundy in France. The area's ancient Kimmeridgian limestone soils are unique and produce fine, pristine, mineral-like white wines made out of Burgundy's white star, Chardonnay. With the use of new oak largely frowned upon in Chablis, the best examples display soft stone/ citrus fruit, honey, river-rock, hay, mineral, and cashew character. Trademark mouthwatering acidity ensures that the best examples are with us for years.

Chardonnay
(SHAR-do-nay)

Love it or loathe it, you can't deny this grape its place in wine's hall of fame. Some of the very best examples hail from Burgundy, where texture, finesse, structure, and aging ability rule over simple "drink-now" fruit flavors. You see, Chardonnay comes in all different shapes and sizes. Flavors range from the delicate, citrus, and slightly honeyed styles of Chablis to warmer, southern-hemisphere styles, where aromas range from peaches and pears to full-throttle, ripe tropical fruits like banana, pineapple, guava, and mango.

Chenin Blanc
(shuh-nin blon)

Handier than a Swiss army knife, the globetrotting Chenin's high natural acidity and tendency to flirt with botrytis lend it equally well to a variety of styles: sweet, dry, or fizzy. A good traveler, Chenin's original stamping ground is France's Loire Valley, where it makes racy dry whites, luscious sweet wines, and clean, frothy fizz. Expect aromas of apples, gooseberries, and fresh herbs.

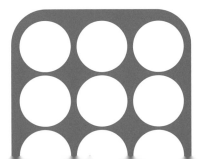

Gewurztraminer

(geh-verz-tra-mee-ner)

Like a drag queen with too much makeup and perfume (and little shame), this is the incredibly camp member of the white grape family. In reality, Gewurz is one of the superstar varieties of Alsace in France. The best ooze aromas of litchi, rose, orange blossom, cinnamon, ginger, and spice. Good Gewurz will be rich and weighty, with great length of flavor.

Marsanne

Clean, fresh, and fruity, this grape plays second fiddle to Viognier in France's northern Rhône Valley; however, it dominates many of the white wine blends of the southern Rhône. Expect ripe, peachy fruit flavors, fresh acidity, and barely a whiff of oak. With a bit of age, Marsanne takes on an amazing honeyed character and becomes slightly oilier, with more weight and richness. Outside France, you might see it in parts of Australia.

Muscat

For the purposes of this book, the large Muscat family of grapes can be split into non-identical triplets: Muscat Blanc à Petits Grains, Muscat of Alexandria, and Muscat Ottonel. Wine styles vary from light, fizzy Moscato d'Asti (northwest Italy) and sweet, spirity Muscat de Beaumes-de-Venise (France's Rhône Valley) to Spain's aromatic Málagas and the unique liqueur Muscats of Australia's northeast Victoria.

Palomino Fino

(pal-o-mee-no fee-no)

The most important variety in the production of sherry, accounting for four of the five main styles: manzanilla, fino, amontillado, and oloroso. Fino is the most popular and one of the greatest food wines in the world. The best are bone-dry, nutty, and slightly salty, with great mineral texture and a clean, tangy finish.

Pedro Ximénez
(pay-dro hee-may-neth)

Although "PX," as it's more commonly called, falls into the white grape family, this sun-loving variety produces sweet, thick, syrupy wines. Great examples are almost black in color, viscous, and super-sweet, with intense aromas of raisin and spice.

Pinot Gris/Pinot Grigio
(pee-no gree/pee-no gree-jee-o)

Technically, these are the same grape; the key difference lies in the style. Pinot Grigio tends to be light, delicate, and fresh, usually made in stainless-steel tanks and best drunk young, when it's zippy and vibrant. Pinot Gris is fatter and richer, with more weight and intensity, often from time spent in oak. Pinot Grigio is commonly found in the cool of northeast Italy, while Pinot Gris is never more happy than in its classic "home," the French region of Alsace. There are also some fabulously aromatic examples emerging from New Zealand nowadays, perfect for fusion and Thai-style dishes, and shellfish too.

Riesling
(rees-ling)

Technically brilliant, but still a wee bit nerdy, Riesling currently represents some of this planet's great bargain wine buys. While its spiritual home is Germany, you'll find world-class examples from Austria, France, and Australia. The best will have beautiful, pure, citrus fruit aromas alongside fresh-cut flowers and spice, with flavors of lemons, limes, and minerals.

Sauvignon Blanc
(so-vin-yon blon)

Think passion fruit, gooseberry, elderflower, black currant... even cat's pee! France, South Africa, Chile, and Australia all have a good crack at it, but New Zealand (Marlborough, to be exact) has become the modern home of this variety. The best examples are pale, unmistakably pungent on the nose, painfully crisp, and ultra-refreshing with plenty of zip and racy acidity.

Semillon

(sem-ee-yon)

Sémillon is native to Bordeaux in France, but it's down under in New South Wales's Hunter Valley that Semillon (note the lack of accent on the "e") has had greatest success, producing beautifully crafted and insanely long-lived wines. In its youth, great examples explode with pear, white peach, and other ripe summer fruits. But stash a bottle away for a rainy day a few years down the line and you'll witness this variety's true magic: aromas of super-intense citrus fruit—even marmalade—alongside toast, honey, nuts, and sweet spice.

Sherry

Sherry is the English term for the wine-producing region of Jerez-de-la-Frontera in Spain's Andalucia. There are a number of styles produced in the sherry-producing triangle over there, and from a number of different varieties. Wine styles can run anywhere from bone-dry to super-sweet, while the key grape varieties used to produce them are Palomino Fino, Pedro Ximénez, and Moscatel.

Verdicchio

(vehr-dik-ee-o)

Verdicchio is grown and produced in Italy's central Marche region, and can make everything from light, crisp whites to big, rich ones. All are pretty neutral when it comes to aroma, but super-lemony in flavor, with the best showing plenty of spice and richness. Because of their weight, the full-bodied examples can handle oak too, so expect to see some wooded examples.

Viognier

(vee-on-yee-ay)

Viognier overflows with intoxicating aromas of apricots, orange rind, and fresh-cut flowers. It's weighty, rich, and oily in texture, with great length and beautifully soft acidity. Native to France's northern Rhône, it also shows promise in Australia and South Africa.

The Reds

Cabernet Sauvignon
(kab-er-nay so-veen-yon)

King of the red grapes, the best display power, finesse, elegance, the ability to age, and universal appeal. Its home was Bordeaux, but particularly good examples now also come from Italy, Spain, Chile, Argentina, South Africa, Australia, and California. The range of flavors and aromas varies greatly, but look for black currant, dark cherry, and plummy fruit alongside cedar, mint, and eucalyptus.

Carmenère
(car-men-yair)

Carmenère can be a nightmare in the vineyard: it's hard to get ripe, and once it is, you have a tiny window in which to pick it before the acidity disappears. But when it's good, it's really good! Bearing an uncanny likeness to Merlot, the best examples are bursting with super-dark fruits (plums, blackberries, and black cherries) and aromas of spice and leather.

Chianti
(ki-AN-tee)

Chianti is a region in Tuscany made up of eight distinct sub-districts, including the key ones of Colli Senesi, Classico, and Rufina. It circles the city of Florence and extends toward Sienna in the south. There are eight grape varieties permitted for use in Chianti, although few producers nowadays use all eight (some of which are white), with many preferring to focus on Tuscany's native red star, Sangiovese. Increasingly, Merlot, Cabernet Sauvignon, and Syrah are being used to "bulk up" Sangiovese's often lean and skeletal frame.

Grenache
(grin-ash)

Grown widely in Spain, France, and Australia, Grenache is the workhorse of red grapes, and can be a stand-alone performer in its own right. As concentrated, weighty, fully-fledged reds (especially in France's southern Rhône), the wines sit comfortably alongside some of the world's greatest. Grenache also provides the base for many rosés: its low tannin, acidity, and good whack of alcohol go perfect in pink.

Malbec

This red grape variety loves the sun and is found in Argentina's Andes Mountains (home to a handful of the highest-altitude vineyards on earth). These are often big wines, and the best are soft and super-fruity, with fantastically perfumed aromas of violets and lavender along with plenty of plums and spice.

Merlot
(mer-low)

Merlot has long played second fiddle to Big Brother Cabernet, often being sidelined for blending, and yet it's the most widely planted red grape in Bordeaux, and in recent times both California and Australia have developed a love affair with it. New World examples tend to be plump, with ripe, plummy fruit and naturally low tannin. Wines from north of the equator are drier, leaner, and generally less in your face.

Mourvèdre
(more-ved-rah)

The star of the southern Rhône. Along with dark, sweet fruit there's mushroom, tobacco, roast lamb—even the elephant pen at the zoo! In Spain it's known as Monastrell and Mataró, while in Australia it's also known as Mataro. Because of its funkiness, it rarely appears solo and is usually reserved for blending.

Nebbiolo
(neb-ee-yo-lo)

The best examples of Nebbiolo are layered and complex, oozing aromas of tar, roses, dark cherry, black olives, and rosemary. In great wines, concentrated fruit, firm acidity, and a wash of drying tannins ensure that they'll go the distance if you want to stash them away. Nebbiolo's home is Piedmont, where it stacks up to everything, from mushrooms to chicken, rabbit, all sorts of game —even good old, moldy cheeses.

Pinot Noir

(pee-no nwar)

Top examples of Pinot are seductive, intriguing, even sexy, and their versatility with food is near unrivaled. Thought of as one of the lightest reds, top examples show layers of strawberry, raspberry, plum, and dark forest fruits, with aromas of earth, spice, animal, cedar, and truffle. These wines range from delicate and minerally to silky and rich. Try those from the Côte de Nuits in Burgundy, and New Zealand's Central Otago and Martinborough regions.

Primitivo / Zinfandel

(prim-i-tee-vo / zin-fvan-del)

For ages we thought these were different varieties, but they're actually the same. Zinfandel ("Zin" for short) is found in the mighty USA, where most things big are seen as beautiful. In southern Italy, Primitivo rides high alongside Negroamaro and Nero d'Avola. With plenty of sweet, ripe fruit and aromas of violets and leather, this style is much more restrained than its transatlantic brother.

Rioja

(ree-O-hah)

Rioja is in northern Spain and best known for its rich, full-flavored reds. Tempranillo is the star grape, although red varieties Garnacha, Graciano, and Mazuelo are also permitted in the blend. Similarly, as a changing of the guard takes place, international varieties such as Cabernet Sauvignon, Merlot, and Syrah are increasingly finding their way into Rioja's modern face.

Rosé

(rose-AY)

It seems everyone has caught onto Rosé's food-friendliness and thirst-slaking credentials. Ranging from palest pink to almost garnet in color, it can be made sweet, dry, or anywhere in between from just about any red grape. The most common way to make good rosé is called the *saignée* method. A bit like making a cup of tea, the skins are left in contact with the juice before fermentation to get the desired level of color, flavor, and tannin. While Provence is making a comeback and California is holding its own, great rosés are emerging from Australia, South America, Spain, and Portugal. Even England has produced some fine examples.

Sangiovese

(san-gee-o-vay-zay)

Loaded with aromas of dark cherry, plum, and forest fruits, Sangiovese often also smells of tobacco, spice, and earth. Most remember its trademark "super-drying" tannins, which, without food, can make this grape a hard slog. It's native to Tuscany, where it shines as Chianti Classico and Brunello di Montalcino. More recently, it has surfaced in both Australia and the USA, but so far without the same success.

Syrah / Shiraz

(sih-rah/sheer-az)

Syrah is the French name for this grape. The style tends to be lighter in body than Shiraz, with aromas of red currants, raspberry, plum, and nearly always white pepper and spice. Shiraz, from Australia and the New World, tends to be concentrated and ripe. At its best, it oozes plum, raspberry, earth, cedar, and freshly ground black pepper. Some New World winemakers are now calling their wines Syrah to reflect the lighter style they are now making.

Tempranillo

(tem-pra-nee-yo)

The grand old man of Spanish wine. Native to Rioja, it has also sunk its roots in nearby Ribera del Duero, Navarra, Priorat, and Toro. Typically, it has a solid core of dark berry fruits complete with a rustic edge that relies on savory aromas such as tobacco, spice, leather, and earth. A recent trend has been to make international styles with big color, big fruit, and big oak.

Touriga Nacional

(too-ree-ga na-ssee-o-nahl)

Touriga plays a starring role in many of Portugal's great fortified wines as well as being a key component in more than a few of its new-wave table wines. Deep, densely fruited, leathery, and with an almost inky texture, Touriga needs time to mellow. Expect to smell dried fruit, leather, and violets, while fortified wines will be richer, stacked with dried-fruit flavor, and boasting much sweetness.

THE HOT
100

Skimp · **Drink** · **Dine** · **Splurge**

25 wines for less

When money's tight, you make sacrifices. You start by trading in your gym membership, you continue by making your morning coffee at home rather than buying it out, those shoes you'd planned to throw away you fix, and the $15 you used to spend on a bottle of wine will soon enough become $10. This chapter lifts the lid on the best wines for as little money as possible. From a spread of countries, regions, varieties, and styles, these are simple wines for Tuesday nights in front of the TV, wines for bringing in the weekend, wines for lazy Sunday afternoons — wines that will soon enough have you saving your travel money and walking to work instead.

Skimp

Powers Winery Cabernet Sauvignon 2007 Columbia Valley Washington State USA

This is a knockout example of Cabernet that provides brilliant everyday drinking at a really affordable price. Closer inspection will reveal a wine that is plush and fruit-driven, and perfectly geared toward those who like their reds richly fruited and ready to drink.

Expect to find wave after wave of sweet black fruit on the nose, while in your mouth it's soft and rich with nicely rounded tannins and a long, dry finish. And while it's great as it is, a couple of nicely charred lamb chops or even just a good old burger would only add to the magic.

get it from...

$$$$$

www.badgermtnvineyard.com

Cellier des Dauphins Prestige Côtes du Rhône 2007
Southern Rhône France

A new injection of energy (and possibly cash) has seen the once-weary wines of the Cellier des Dauphins cooperative return to form. Much of that investment has occurred in the winery, where spotless conditions and plenty of stainless steel provide a great starting point for straight-shooting, fruit-fresh examples such as this.

Delicious ripe raspberry fruit dominates the nose here alongside trademark aromas of southern Rhône bramble and spice. Time in oak is kept to a minimum, but there is enough fruit tannin on board to keep an otherwise amply fruited palate in check.

get it from...

$$$$$

www.frank-lin.com

Souverain Alexander Valley Chardonnay 2008 California USA

Chardonnay rules in the Alexander Valley. The cooler, southern areas together with the inland climate and rich soil help the grapes maintain their trademark acidity and power.

The wine is made in a classic style, pressing whole clusters of grapes, with individual lots being fermented and aged separately in barrel before being blended by top winemaker Ed Killian. The result? A rich, intense style where the wine overflows with layers of apple, pear, and honeyed lemon rind. For such a reasonable price, it delivers a timeless, classic Chardonnay style that truly exceeds expectations.

get it from...

$$$$$

www.souverain.com

Gruet
Brut NV
New Mexico
USA

It doesn't come as any great surprise to me to learn that this *méthode champenoise*-style sparkling wine has seriously wide circulation throughout the USA. As value for money goes, this wine is nothing short of magic. Fresh as a daisy, it is bright, crisp, long, and has real depth of flavor.

The talented Laurent Gruet uses only the free-run juice for his base wines, resulting in wines of real elegance and finesse. If it isn't already, make this wine a regular feature in your refrigerator.

get it from...

$$$$$

www.gruetwinery.com

Charles Smith
Kung Fu Girl
Riesling 2008
Columbia Valley
Washington State
USA

Like many of Charles Smith's wine creations, this label is good fun, but with serious wine inside the bottle. The Kung Fu Girl Riesling features beautifully balanced fruit with just the right amount of keen acidity. The floral and citrus aromatics suggest that the wine is both delicate and agile at the same time.

Charles Smith has a special knack for finding unique vineyard sites and he shapes his concept around this raw material. The prominent mineral components apparent in this wine are no accident. The wine packs a powerful punch and would provide a great pairing for your spicy Szechuan take-out meal. Otherwise, with quite low alcohol levels, you can feel free to enjoy it at lunchtime.

get it from...

$$$$$

www.charlessmithwines.com

Altos
Las Hormigas
Malbec 2008
Mendoza
Argentina

Tough times call for tough measures — which, if you're a carnivore, might mean rethinking your favorite cut of meat. Beef lovers who don't mind a bit of a chew should consider the shank, the rump, or the hanger — all of which pack plenty of flavor at a fraction of the cost.

Grill it simply over coals if you can — or in the pan if you can't — and serve with nothing more than a drizzle of good olive oil, a pinch of sea salt, and a dollop of your favorite mustard. The rugged and user-friendly Altos Las Hormigas Malbec is the ideal sparring partner, with layer upon layer of sweet, dark fruit leading to a full-bodied palate where fruit and oak coexist happily. Dry, grippy tannins will help reduce the chew factor no end.

get it from...

$$$$$

www.skurnikwines.com

Castle Rock Winery Willamette Valley Pinot Noir 2008 Oregon USA

One of the hardest things to put your hands on in the world of wine is great-value Pinot Noir— examples that don't cost an arm and a leg. Harder still is having to produce them. And so you can probably understand my joy at finding this knockout example. Greg Popovich founded Castle Rock back in 1994, his idea being to deliver value-for-money wines. With long-term winemaker Joe Briggs on board, he appears to be bang on target.

Approachable, medium-bodied, and with more than accurate varietal characteristics, expect great depth, a nice even structure, and terrific length of flavor. This would work beautifully with either roast chicken or pork. Aquatarians should look to the best piece of tuna or salmon they can lay their hands on.

get it from...

$$

www.castlerockwinery.com

TOP 20 TIPS
#**01**

Support green

Whenever possible, buy organic, biodynamic, and Fairtrade wines. Do a bit of research to find out who is doing what, or ask at your local wine store, as many producers don't make mention of their green initiatives on their labels. Support those who are making an effort to leave the planet in better shape than they found it.

Bonny Doon
Vin Gris de Cigare
Rosé 2008
California
USA

The world really does need more Randall Grahms. As one of my all-time wine heroes, mainly for his refreshingly welcome — and often eccentric — take on the wine world, Grahm effortlessly knits together serious winemaking with Monty Python-like attitude. His love affair with things European translates into a range of wines that display elegance and refinement, but never at the expense of good fruit.

Grahm blends this rosé from a veritable "fruit salad" of grape varieties, including Grenache, Cinsault, Mourvèdre, and Syrah, plus a couple of whites, Grenache Blanc and Roussanne. The result is a bone-dry, breathtaking wine that should be your new favorite drink of the summer.

get it from...

$$$$

www.bonnydoonvineyard.com

Oxford Landing GSM 2008
Multidistrict blend South Australia

Oh la la! Like Paul Hogan in Lacoste, this straightforward Rhône-a-like blend of Grenache, Shiraz, and Mourvèdre is one of a growing number of its kind and, more importantly, a real breath of fresh air in the often-dreary world of cut-price wine. What makes it even better is the less-is-more approach that sees select parcels of the varieties mentioned above carefully blended to create a medium-bodied, fruit-rich wine minus the influence of oak — a wine that's as happy with food as without. If you need any more convincing, production is overseen by the good folk behind the controls at Yalumba.

get it from...

$$$$$

www.negociantsusa.com

Ampelos
Rosé of Syrah
2008
Santa Barbara
California
USA

Ampelos is the Greek word for vine, reflecting the winery owners' heritage and philosophy that great wines are made in the field. Their 100 percent biodynamic vineyards are also some of only a handful in California that are certified as being sustainably farmed.

Judging by this rosé, the result is absolutely delicious. Made in the classic Provençal style, expect to find soft berry notes bound up in a restrained, focused, mineral, and deftly textured wine. The tannins are silky, soft, and beautifully knitted with the fruit. Outstanding value for money and just the thing for chargrilled shrimp and aioli.

get it from...

$$$$$

www.ampeloscellars.com

Do your bit

Unless you're in the market for a
box of wine, ride your bike to your
local wine store or — better still — walk.
Driving any more than a couple of
miles in your car uses up more CO_2
than shipping a bottle of wine from
Australia to the USA.

Casillero del Diablo
Shiraz Rosé 2008
Central Valley
Chile

Chile is working overtime to shake off its "cheap and cheerful" reputation, with the production of some breathtaking wines from cooler regions. Still, Chile does cheap and cheerful better than just about anybody, and so for that reason — much as I'm excited by the advances being made — I hope they never completely lose the ability to produce the great bargains they do.

This full-throttle dry rosé from Chilean juggernaut Concha y Toro boasts deep color with plenty of dark-berried fruit and subtle spice, both of which are nicely supported by a lick of tannin and cleansing acidity.

get it from...

$$$$$

www.conchaytoro.com

Four Vines
Naked
Chardonnay 2008
Santa Barbara
California
USA

This gem is one of the pillar wines of the irreverent trio that make up the Four Vines team: Chris Tietje, Sam Mahler, and Bill Grant.

Plain and simple, Naked Chardonnay is all about purity of fruit. Made from 100 percent Chardonnay and with zero oak influence, this wine is an essay in balance and freshness. Exercising restraint, here you'll find a nose full of bright citrus and stone fruit, while the palate is tightly wound and delicate, with soft pear and apple notes and a fine, mineral texture. Cool fermentation in stainless steel and none of the softening influence of malolactic fermentation has translated into a truly mouthwatering wine.

get it from...

$$$$$

www.fourvines.com

Crew Wines
Matchbook
Chardonnay 2007
Dunnigan Hills
California
USA

This is one of the wines from Crew Wines — the original talent behind the success of that other Dunnigan Hills pioneer, RH Phillips.

From its compact, lemony nose that includes subtle smells of apple, pear, sweet spice, hazelnut, and minerals to its intense and finely structured palate, this is a great illustration of just how good New World Chardonnay can be. Spending time in new oak barrels and with the inclusion of around 13 percent Russian River fruit and two percent Viognier, the result is a delicious, full-bodied wine that drinks well now and should be enjoyed over the next couple of years. This is just the thing to have hidden in the back of the refrigerator for those lazy Sunday afternoons!

get it from...

**$$**$$

www.crewwines.com

Torres
Sangre de Toro
2007
Penedès
Spain

In my mind, Sangre de Toro has always been unbeatable value. For decades this delicious little wine from Spain's northeast corner has been winning hearts right around the globe for its uncomplicated, easy-drinking style and, dare I say it, for that little black plastic bull that comes attached to the neck of every bottle — which kind of makes it like the adult equivalent of a breakfast cereal novelty.

This straightforward blend of Garnacha and Cariñena minus the influence of oak is rich with aromas of raspberry, smoke, and spice. The palate is soft, forward, and provides delicious everyday drinking — hands down one of the absolute bargains of the year.

get it from...

$$$$$

www.dreyfusashby.com

Four Sisters Sauvignon Blanc 2008
Multidistrict blend Australia

Almost a dozen years ago, Trevor Mast—one of Australia's most knowledgeable and enduring winemakers—launched the Four Sisters range, receiving widespread praise in the process. Today it remains one of the best-value selections of its kind.

Select parcels of Sauvignon Blanc are drawn from a number of cool-climate regions in a bid to produce a bright, herbaceous style, and one that's geared for drinking ASAP. Lean, tight, and well structured, the nose is loaded with smells of passionfruit, green apple, and mown grass, while in the mouth it's vibrant, zippy, and bone-dry.

get it from...

**$$**$$$

www.foursisters.com.au

Chateau St Jean Fumé Blanc 2008 Sonoma County California USA

Dry, crisp Sauvignon Blanc that has juicy citrus fruit at this price is a home run. This is fantastic value for a wine that shows true complexity, balance, and finesse. To see these traditional characteristics in a New World, fumé-styled wine encourages me.

With its medium body, this Chateau St Jean Fumé Blanc will please those who prefer a slightly fuller texture and style. It is a great afternoon wine and will go particularly well with shellfish or something like a goat cheese salad.

get it from...

$$\$\$$$

www.chateaustjean.com

TOP 20 TIPS

#**03**

Shop sensibly

PET, Tetra, and lightweight glass are all better for the environment. Do a bit of research to find out who is using them and support those brands.

Château Guiot Rosé Costières de Nîmes 2008 Provence France

Sandwiched between the Languedoc, Provence, and the Rhône, the precariously stony soils of the Costières de Nîmes provide a near-perfect environment in which to grow grapes. Locals François and Sylvia Cornut run the much-loved 300-acre (120-hectare) Château Guiot, with François in charge of the vineyards and Sylvia the winery.

Grenache, Syrah, and Cinsault are the stars here, and produce a lush, juicy red and one of only two rosés I'd consider walking over hot coals for. Encompassing all three varieties, expect a nose crammed with raspberry, red currant, and dried-herb aromas, while a fresh, fruity palate gives way to crunchy acidity and a clean, drying finish.

get it from...

$$\$\$\$\$

www.robertkacherselections.com

Heitz Cellars Ink Grade Port NV Napa Valley California USA

Back in the early nineties, second generation winemaker David Heitz became inspired following his travels through Portugal. The result? This brilliant effort, where plantings of a number of Portuguese grapes in the renowned Ink Grade Vineyard produce a traditional fortified wine.

Composed of several older vintages along with some more recent vintages that add perk and vibrancy, expect a concentrated and power-packed port with a nose of dried fig, dark plum, and bitter chocolate. In your mouth it's inky and rich, with masses of intensity and a clean, beautifully balanced finish. Drink it with some blue-veined cheese or alongside dark chocolate anything!

get it from...

$$ $$$ (375ml)

www.heitzcellar.com

Peter Lehmann Clancy's Red 2006 Barossa Valley Australia

On the subject of great-value drinking, it would be remiss of me not to mention a wine that, despite its more than reasonable price tag, has been included in *Wine Spectator*'s Top 100 on no less than four occasions.

With access to some of the best old vineyards in the Barossa Valley, Peter Lehmann's Clancy's combines Shiraz, Cabernet Sauvignon, and Merlot with a dash of Cabernet Franc to deliver a soft, plush, fruit-driven red that is designed for early consumption. In the winery, fermentation on skins lasts around seven days, prior to the wine being processed, clarified, and then matured in a combination of French and American oak for around 12 months.

get it from...

$$$$

www.peterlehmannwines.com

Chivite
Gran Feudo
Rosado 2007
Navarra
Spain

As all-time wine bargains go, this is one of the best. For millions of years (okay, so not millions of years, but a long time nevertheless) Chivite has produced this bright-as-a-button, fruit-driven rosé from high up in Spain's northeast corner, where drinking rosé is as macho as running with bulls.

Like most examples from Navarra, Grenache is the star of this show and provides both the framework and the appropriate stuffing required to produce delicious rosé. Smells and flavors range from raspberry and wild strawberry through to ripe red apples and spice, all of which are nicely supported by a lick of tannin and a snappy, drying finish.

get it from...

$$ $$

www.kobrandwineandspirits.com

Drink local

Wines from local
vineyards have
had to travel less.
This is a good thing.

Vallis Mareni
Ombra
Prosecco NV
Veneto
Italy

Given the choice, a glass of really good Prosecco—of which there are few—is always a far better proposition than a really average glass of Champagne—of which there are far too many. Luckily, there has been a noticeable rise in the amount of good Prosecco coming forward, one of which is Ombra.

Prosecco grapes are fermented to form base wines, blended, and then re-fermented in large tanks prior to bottling under pressure. The result in this case is a clean, modern wine with aromas of lemon rind, green apple, and honeysuckle. The palate is softer and less gassy than most sparkling wines, and best of all it weighs in for a third of the price of most average Champagnes.

get it from...

$$$$$

www.omniwines.com

Telmo Rodríguez
Al Muvedre 2008
Alicante
Spain

The Telmo Rodríguez approach is not an uncommon one: respect the past, believe in the future, do things as naturally as you can, intervene as little as possible, and let the identity of the place speak for itself via the finished product. With this in mind, Al Muvedre is a down-to-earth, young, unoaked red from the tiny Valencian DO of Alicante, designed to be drunk now.

Aromas range from dark-berried fruits through to smoke, earth, and ground dried spice. There's nice weight on the palate also, where after a wash of sweet cherryish fruit, a wave of fine, chewy tannins finishes things off.

get it from...

$$$$$$

www.vintuswines.com

Share your wine

Drink wine with other people. Get a group of friends together, open a whole load of bottles, plonk them in the middle of the table, taste, talk, listen, and laugh — it's another great way to learn about wine.

Catena Alamos Chardonnay 2008 Mendoza Argentina

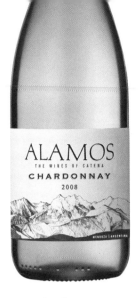

The luxurious suckling pig is one of those versatile wine dishes that can go either way. Its sweet, tender meat and salty crackling is perfectly suited to a range of medium-bodied, dry, grippy reds, or equally at home with a cast of full-flavored, spicy whites. As a diehard Chardonnay fan, I'm always up for option B.

Tucked neatly into the foothills of the Andes Mountains, Argentine powerhouse Catena produces a brilliant style of Chardonnay that speaks volumes about texture, finesse, elegance, and structure, and, most importantly, without leaving you feeling as though you've been gnawing on a piece of lumber. Aromas here are of grapefruit, marzipan, and cashew, while in your mouth it's incredibly long, full, spicy, and dry.

get it from...

$$$$$

www.catenawines.com

Hess Chardonnay 2007 Monterey California USA

After a long overdue makeover, Chardonnay is back. Gone is the once golden appearance, the flabby fruit, the charry oak, and the everything-but-the-kitchen-sink approach that used to turn so many of us away in droves. Chardonnay c. 2010–11, it would seem, has finally learned how to look good naked.

Taken from the cool Shirtail Vineyard in Monterey, this example from Swiss visionary Donald Hess is a great illustration of Chardonnay's new breed. Aromatics range from grapefruit to nectarine, while the palate shows soft citrus fruit, mineral texture, and terrific length of flavor.

get it from...

$$ $$$

www.hesscollection.com

Telmo Rodríguez
Basa Blanco 2008
Rueda
Spain

With this wine consistently ranking as one of the bargains of the year, the Telmo Rodríguez stable knows how to do style and value better than most. This box-fresh blend of Verdejo, Viura, and Sauvignon Blanc will have you scratching your head in amazement at how on earth it continues to charge such reasonable prices for such knockout wines.

Basa — or base as it translates — is the keenly priced white star of the Rodríguez stable, and it's a great place to start. Expect aromas of gooseberry, lemon, and fresh spring peas to hit you with in-your-face intensity. The palate is zippy, clean as a whistle, and packed with restrained passion fruit/lemony flavor.

get it from...

**$$**$$

www.vintuswines.com

25 wines for food

Food glorious food, and made even better in this chapter by well-chosen wine. Like a romantic night in with your better half, food and wine matching shouldn't be an exercise wheeled out only on special occasions, and nor does it need to be expensive or time consuming. Some of the best combinations are also some of the cheapest and easiest to reproduce. And whether you choose to follow the rules or break them all, at the very heart of it, good food and wine matching knits a little bit of art with a little bit of science and a lot of trial and error. Practice makes perfect — *bon appétit!*

Dine

Leitz
Dragonstone
Riesling Kabinett 2008
Mosel
Germany

There is a recipe from food writer and über-cook Nigel Slater that has become a firm winter favorite in our house. It takes chunks of fatty pork belly and renders them down for hours with plenty of onions, butter, lemons, parsley, and capers. It's a completely delicious and sticky dish — even if it's a tad unhealthy; a dish that is literally built for great Riesling.

From one of Germany's brightest young stars comes this textbook example of great modern Riesling. Fresh and limey, with further aromas of sweet spice, ginger, and summer flowers. In the mouth it's delicate, just a little bit sweet, and beautifully balanced by mineral texture and super-fresh acidity. Don't attempt a pork-belly casserole without it!

get it from...

$$$$$

www.skurnikwines.com

Copain
Tous Ensemble
Viognier 2008
Mendocino
California
USA

The talented Wells Guthrie has worked with an impressive, all-star lineup that includes the likes of Chave, Chapoutier, and Turley.

Currently the full-time owner and winemaker for Copain wines in Mendocino, Guthrie is particularly keen on Rhône varieties. His Tous Ensemble — or "All Together," as he calls it — is a beautiful, floral example of Viognier, where bright peach and apricot fruit dominate the nose, while a soft and clean palate that's not at all heavy is nicely framed by gentle acidity and a great length of flavor. As great matches go, stop at slow roast loin of pork rolled and stuffed with dried apricots, chestnuts, and thyme. Serve it with nothing more than a simple green salad and a decent spoonful of salsa verde.

get it from...

$$$$$

www.copainwines.com/tous

Schramsberg Mirabelle Brut Rosé NV North Coast California USA

Cool-climate Chardonnay and Pinot Noir combine here to create one of America's most iconic sparkling wines.

With fruit sourced from both Carneros and the Anderson Valley, Mirabelle follows in the footsteps of Champagne's finest, including strict hand-picking of fruit, stringent sorting at the winery, gentle pressing, and two years on the lees. The result is a dry, complex, and flavorful *cuvée* that is just the ticket for your next special occasion.

get it from...

$$$$$

www.schramsberg.com

Kunin Wines
Paso Robles
Westside Zinfandel 2007
California
USA

Former restaurateur Seth Kunin combines his extensive trade experience with a taste for things "Old World" to create a brilliant range of Euro-styled wines built from top-shelf New World fruit. Sourcing and blending fruit from half a dozen or so vineyard sites, Kunin manages to produce wines that retain both body and intensity, but not at the expense of charm and elegance.

The "Westside" Zinfandel features powerful, sweet black fruits coupled with fine, controlled tannins and a judicious use of oak. A wine like this needs food with soul — slow-cooked meat that's been given a chance to gently bubble and blip away in a pot full of veggies and wine for hours on end. A dish that simply oozes flavor once it's done. That's the kind of food for a wine like this.

get it from...

$$$$$

www.kuninwines.com

Bodegas Hidalgo
La Gitana
Amontillado Napoleon
Jerez
Spain

While Hidalgo's knockout popular La Gitana Manzanilla has become a regular fixture in my refrigerator, it's the dry Napoleon amontillado from the premium range that's really grabbed my attention this year. And I can't believe that it's escaped my notice until now!

Dry, nutty, and complex, this is sherry for serving at room temperature, sherry for drinking with things like smoked fish and salty cured meats, sherry for savoring. A copper color leads to a dry, nutty nose charged with aromas of cedar, smoke, and spice, while in your mouth it's bright and citrus-like, before descending into a long, drying, nutty finish.

get it from...

$$$$$ (500 ml)

www.hidalgoimports.com

Westerly Vineyards Sauvignon Blanc 2007
Santa Ynez
California
USA

The smell of spring in the air should have you automatically reaching for Sauvignon Blanc. This season's ingredients are made for this variety, and while any number of variations on fava beans, peas, mint, basil, lemon, sea salt, and really good peppery olive oil are perfectly suited to Sauvignon Blanc, it's good old goat cheese that creates one of the best matches.

This stylish example from the stony soils of Santa Ynez would be spot on. While a big sniff will reveal classic grapefruit, gooseberry, and mineral character, the palate is dry, tight, and beautifully balanced by mouthwatering acidity and great length of flavor. It would pair very well with Asian-influenced dishes such as snap-fried salt and pepper squid or big, juicy tempura shrimp.

get it from...

$$$$$

www.westerlyvineyards.com

Do things by halves

Half bottles can often provide some amazing value, not to mention the fact that they mature more quickly than a full bottle. Half bottles are also a great alternative to buying wines by the glass, which can sometimes suffer after the pouring bottle has been open for a while.

Westrey
Pinot Noir 2007
Willamette Valley
Oregon
USA

Pinot Noir is incredibly versatile with food. From raw tuna to trout, mushrooms, truffles, chicken, lamb, rabbit, hare, quail, squab, teal, grouse, pheasant, pigeon, partridge, duck, and even salmon, the possibiilites for great matches are seemingly endless. It's an almost spiritual relationship. At best both are rich, decadent, and have terrific intensity of flavor and delicate textures. Together they provide a spellbinding combination.

Traditional winemaking by Amy Wesselman and David Autrey allows the beautiful, expressive fruit drawn from an exceptional vintage in Oregon to really shine through. Hand-harvested, spontaneous natural fermentation, minimal handling, and no fining, the end result is a wine that is multilayered, super-silky, incredibly pure, and little short of magic.

get it from...

**$$$**$$

www.westrey.com

Ponzi
Arneis 2008
Willamette Valley
Oregon
USA

The trailblazing Ponzi family first planted Arneis cuttings in its Oregon vineyard back in 1991, having encountered this varietal when visiting friends in the Piedmont region of northern Italy. They were intrigued by the flavor profile and decided to experiment in their own vineyards.

The grapes have been traditionally pressed in whole clusters and the juice fermented in steel. Like the wines they found in Piedmont, the Ponzi Arneis is expressive and well balanced. The apple, melon, and spiced-pear flavors are garnished with a hint of citrus rind, providing the wine with a lick of tartness during its lengthy finish. This Arneis is delightful to enjoy with fruit and cheese, grilled fish, or even with a simple salad.

get it from...

$$$$$

www.ponziwines.com

Henry of Pelham Special Select Late Harvest Vidal 2007 Ontario Canada

This sweet wine is made from grapes from selected Niagara vineyards The harvest occurs during extremely cold conditions, any time from late November through to the end of January, depending on the readiness of the grapes.

In the winery, the fruit is fermented in stainless-steel tanks, resulting in a wine that is rich, balanced, and vibrant, with smells that range from sweet citrus marmalade through to intense dried apricot. And while dried fruits and full-flavored hard cheeses make for happy matches here, the best combination involves little more than the best lemon tart you can possibly lay your hands on.

get it from...

$$$$$ (37.5 cl)

www.henryofpelham.com

Ask away

Ask your sommelier. Ask the
girl behind the counter of your
local wine store. Ask the guy
at the winery. No matter how
stupid you think your questions
may be, ask away. This is how
you will learn more about wine.

Roederer Estate Brut NV Anderson Valley USA

This is the first, and much underrated, sparkling wine produced in the USA by the iconic Champagne house of Louis Roederer. Okay, so Cristal it's not, but blended from four distinct vineyards of varying soil types and altitudes, this is a very real essay in style and value, where Chardonnay — some of which has spent a bit of time in oak — takes the lead.

Expect to find smells and flavors of fresh bread, marzipan, and rich citrus marmalade, while in the mouth it's long, fine, and packed with all the TLC you'd expect from one of Champagne's greatest names.

get it from...

$$$$$

www.mmdusa.net

Lazy Creek Vineyards Gewürztraminer 2007
Anderson Valley
California
USA

This exotic Gewürztraminer ticks all the right boxes with its rich intensity and clean, balanced vibrancy. Taken mainly from old vines, it has textbook litchi, rose water, and musk notes. The palate too is rich without being fat, with good focus and balance. If you're looking for something to eat with this and have access to decent fish, try steaming a whole snapper or sea bass together with ginger, chili, scallion, cilantro, and soy. Delicious!

get it from...

$$$$$

www.lazycreekvineyards.com

Charles Joguet
Les Petites Roches
Chinon 2007
Loire
France

Charles Joguet redefined how things were done in Chinon. In the vineyard the Cabernet Franc master reduced yields, harvested by hand, and picked only into small crates in a bid to protect and preserve the fruit, while in the winery he fermented in stainless steel rather than concrete, and was a big advocate for site-driven wines rather than blends.

One of the less expensive Joguet wines, Les Petites Roches is a fresh and lively example of Cabernet Franc taken from 30- to 40-year-old vines in the gravelly northwest of Chinon. Bright raspberry and red currant fruit dominate alongside aromas of smoke and earth. The palate is plump, mineral, and fine, with dry, chalky tannins and a clean, balanced finish. Pot-roasted lamb with white beans, garlic, and rosemary is a classic match here.

get it from...

$$$$$

www.kermitlynch.com

Millton Vineyards Te Arai Chenin Blanc 2007 Gisborne New Zealand

James and Annie Millton established the Millton Vineyard in Gisborne in 1984, having returned from working in the vineyards of Europe. Champions of the biodynamic movement, the Milltons produce a range of wines via sound ecological practices that ensure the balance and health of their vineyards and all things within. The Te Arai vineyards lie just three miles from the sea and provide a happy hunting ground for Chenin Blanc, with mist from the Te Arai waterways encouraging some botrytis activity.

Expect to find crème brûlée, cashew, grapefruit, nectarine, and pork rind on the nose, while in your mouth it's rich and intense with mineral texture and jawdropping length of flavor.

get it from...

$$$$$

www.robertbathimports.com

Vesevo
Greco di Tufo 2008
Campania
Italy

Friday night is pizza night in the Skinner house. If we're feeling motivated we'll make them from scratch, covering the kitchen in flour as we go, otherwise we'll just order them in. Whichever we choose, the topping combinations seem to stay pretty consistent: tomato, mozzarella, capers and anchovy, salami and fresh chili, potato and rosemary, or the tried and tested classic, the Margarita.

And yes, while we know the best pizza wines are usually red, this delicious white from the chilly hills of Campania is right up to the task. Pure and racy, with a nose that's rich with aromas of lemon, beeswax, and marzipan, while in your mouth expect rounded citrus fruit bound by lovely mineral texture.

get it from...

$$$$$

www.vindivino.com

Planeta
Rosé 2008
Sicily
Italy

There's freshness to Sicilian food that, no matter where you are or how cold it may be, literally makes you want to pick up your plate and move outside. In short, this is food that reminds you of eating outdoors — food that reminds you of summer.

Start with a couple of squares of sheeps' milk ricotta, and then for the salad combine a couple of small, sweet tomatoes halved and then quartered, a few salted capers, black olives, a handful each of fresh cilantro and spearmint leaves, then a few drops of red wine vinegar, a pinch of sea salt, and good olive oil to finish. Planeta Rosato 2008 is the perfect partner. Made from 100 percent Syrah and sourced from Sicily's northwest corner, it is fruit-fresh and bone dry, and outstanding value for money.

get it from...

$$$$$

www.palmbay.com

Bründlmayer Grüner Veltliner Kamptaler Terrassen 2008 Kamptal Austria

The Bründlmayer estate employs sound ecological practices with a definite nod to organic and biodynamic farming. No chemical fertilizers, herbicides, pesticides, or fungicides are used in the vineyards, and when old vines are removed, the soil is given a minimum of five years to regenerate. This is rich and racy Grüner from arguably Austria's largest fine winegrowing area, the Kamptal, carrying aromas and flavors of white peach, wet wool, and spice.

With Riesling occupying the best of the higher sites within the area, the lower-altitude, clay-rich soils closer to the Danube River provide the perfect spot for the cultivation of Grüner Veltliner. A stunning illustration of just how good this estate is.

get it from...

$$$$$

www.skurnikwines.com

Wine is for drinking

It's easy to fall into the trap of
buying wine to keep and then
never getting around to drinking
it before it starts its downward
slide. Don't get too precious
about your bottles — open and
share them.

Concha y Toro Late Harvest Sauvignon Blanc 2006 Maule Valley Chile

I'm a sucker for a good pavlova and luckily my mother-in-law makes one of the best. It comes with a thick meringue base about the size of a 12-inch record, followed by a layer of cream, and then another slightly smaller layer of meringue, more cream, and then finally an explosion of fresh passion fruit pulp and big, sweet strawberry halves. It's a sight to behold — but nowhere near as impressive as the spectacle of me trying to force a slice into my mouth. Fortunately, suitable wine matches are in abundance, and this star from Chilean powerhouse Concha y Toro is perfect.

On the nose expect pretty pineapple, honey, and candied citrus fruits, while in your mouth it's fresh — not at all cloying — clean, and lively, with great concentration and length.

get it from...

**$$**$$$ (500 ml)

www.skurnikwines.com

Perrin & Fils Cairanne Côtes du Rhône Villages Peyre Blanche 2007 Southern Rhône France

Take it from me. The odd token bottle of wine goes a long way with most good butchers. Far enough that in many cases they'll not only happily cut you multiple slices of wafer-thin veal scallop — an annoying job at the best of times — but happily offer to pound them flat for you too.

And that matters because the schnitzel is back, a dish that besides being ridiculously easy to produce (provided you've got a kind-natured butcher) is also really wine friendly. As a rule, medium-bodied reds with minimal oak will serve you best, and this bright and breezy offering from southern Rhône star Perrin would be spot on.

get it from...

$$$$$

www.vineyardbrands.com

Fonseca
Unfiltered LBV Port 2003
Douro
Portugal

Good wine and cheese matches aren't as difficult to produce as you might imagine, largely because you're combining two finished products. First consider texture — light and delicate, soft and creamy, hard and dry, heavy and intense — balancing the weight of both your wine and cheese as evenly as possible is step one.

Also consider flavor — generally the more flavor you have in your cheese, the more flavor you'll need in your wine. Acidity is important too. It's no great coincidence that high-acid cheeses such as fresh goat cheese work beautifully with high-acid wines such as young Sauvignon Blanc. And finally consider mold — mold can often make dry wines seem fruitless and bitter. To this end, port and Stilton is one of the all-time classic combinations. Try it!

get it from...

$$$$$

www.kobrandwineandspirits.com

Campbells Rutherglen Muscat NV Rutherglen Australia

Australia's fortified wines are unique in the sense that they represent a little slice of liquid history. They're wines that have kept drinkers smiling for well in excess of 130 years, yet sadly they never quite get the consumer recognition they deserve. The process from start to finish is long and laborious, and finished wines are often left to mature for decades. Relative to the cost of production, Australia's fortified wines represent some of the wine world's last great bargains and some of the best things to drink with food.

This example sits atop a pile of truly mind-blowing Aussie fortifieds. With the constituent wines having an average age of 12 years but drawing on blending material far older, this is pure and concentrated dried-raisin fruit, mocha, and exotic spice, complete with a beautifully textured palate, fresh acidity, and a long, sweet finish.

get it from...

$$$$$ (375 ml)

www.clickwinegroup.com

Concha y Toro Terrunyo Sauvignon Blanc 2008
Casablanca Chile

Terrunyo — the Spanish word for the French word *terroir* that has no straight-forward English translation. Confused? Strange as it might sound, a combination of gravelly soils coupled with the cooling breezes of the Pacific Ocean make the area of Casablanca ideal for the production of A-grade Sauvignon Blanc. Apart from just the faintest hint of green in the glass, any trace of color is virtually non-existent.

The nose is a different story altogether, with intense smells of passion fruit, gooseberry, and black currant alongside those of fresh-cut grass and spring peas. The palate is fruity, fresh, clean, crisp, and mineral.

get it from...

$$$$$

www.conchaytoro.com

Serve it at the right temperature

More often than not we serve white wine too cool and red wine not cool enough. If it is served at the wrong temperature, you risk changing the aromatics, the flavors, and the textures of a wine. And while 20 minutes in the freezer is okay, the microwave is definitely out of bounds.

Codorníu
Pinot Noir
Brut Rosé NV
Penedès
Spain

I've said it before, but there's something very liberating about a picnic on the beach, toes in the sand, sun on its way down, decent company, and a good bottle of bubbles within arm's reach. Wines with plenty of acidity and bubbles really come into their own here, working hard to clean and refresh your palate.

From Spanish bubbles giant Codorníu, this utterly mouthwatering Rose Cava made from 100 percent Pinot Noir has an attractive nose of fresh summer berries and a palate that's both lively and well structured.

get it from...

$$$$$

www.codorniu.es

d'Arenberg
The Noble Riesling 2007
McLaren Vale
Australia

d'Arenberg has been growing grapes in McLaren Vale for near enough 100 years. For many moons it was a supplier of grapes to South Australia's bigger players, but by the late 1920s it had decided to go it alone, turning at least some of its attention to making wine too. Today, as then, vineyards are dry-farmed, minimal sprays are used, and everything that can be done by hand is. Winemaking is handled by Chester Osborn, the fourth-generation member of the d'Arenberg clan.

The Noble Riesling is named after the botrytis fungus — a.k.a. noble rot — that causes the grapes to shrivel and concentrate their sweetness. Expect a nose overflowing with ripe stone fruit, sweet orange marmalade, and spice, while the palate is bright and full but not cloying, with a long, crisp finish.

get it from...

$$$$$$ (375 ml)

www.oldbridgecellars.com

Louis M Martini
Sonoma County
Cabernet Sauvignon 2007
Sonoma Valley
California
USA

This Cabernet was made at the St Helena winery, which the Martini family built at the end of the Prohibition era. At that time Louis Martini had already established himself as a talented grape-grower and winemaker. While he traveled back to Italy to study winemaking, he became particularly enamored with the Cabernet Sauvignon grapes that thrived in his family's Napa and Sonoma vineyards.

Over 140,000 cases of this modern, well-priced Cabernet Sauvignon are made. For such a large-scale production, the wine displays classic Cabernet blackberry and concentrated black currant fruit character. Both voluptuous and dense, there are cedar, anise, and vanilla flavors also to be found, while the palate displays nice, integrated tannins, earth tones, and fine, even layers on the finish.

get it from...

www.louismartini.com

Let it breathe

With the exception of the classics, few wines being produced today need to breathe for a long time. Having said that, get yourself a decanter and decant everything; all reds and most full-bodied whites will benefit from a quick burst of oxygen 10–15 minutes before you plan to serve them.

J L Wolf
Wachenheimer
Riesling 2007
Pfalz
Germany

Ernie Loosen, our esteemed Producer of the year, is a busy man. Multiple collaborations aside, he also runs two successful domaines — Dr Loosen in the Mosel and J L Wolf in the Pfalz. While the J L Wolf history extends back over 200 years, it's the last ten from which the significant advances have come.

Having taken control of the estate in 1996, Loosen quickly set about training his focus on the J L Wolf vineyards. The results are amazing. From the village vineyard series, the Wachenheimer Riesling is one of those classic wines in which acidity and sweetness coexist without effort. Expect a pretty nose of lime zest and fresh spring flowers, while in your mouth it's delicate, fine, and just this side of dry.

get it from...

$$$$$

www.jlwolf.com

25 wines for living

Friends are coming for dinner, you're celebrating a pay rise, there's a birthday that needs toasting, maybe it's a night out at your favorite local restaurant, a day at the races, a romantic picnic for two — whatever the occasion, you'll be better off with a decent bottle of wine on standby. In this chapter we shine the light on the wines that consistently over-deliver given what they'll set you back. Great as they are, these aren't wines for hoarding under your bed, or treating like they're the last bottles you're ever going to own — these are wines for drinking now and, better still, for sharing.

Drink

Domaine Chandon
Blanc de Noirs NV
Multidistrict blend
California
USA

Chandon is the northern California outpost of Champagne Goliath Moët & Chandon, established in 1973 in a bid to create world-class sparkling wine drawing heavily on Champagne techniques. Traditionally, it has headlined red Champagne grapes (Pinots Noir and Meunier) in its *blanc de noirs*. Highly regarded, it's been the sparkler of choice for years for receptions held at the White House.

Ripe, dark-cherry fruit with rich, full texture abound and are the result of a long growing season for these red grapes. Winemaker Tom Tiburzi highlights the flexible nature of the wine and notes that it works perfectly with delicate cuisine, but is also up to the challenge of matching more heavily spiced dishes.

get it from...

**$$$**$$

www.southernwine.com

Elk Cove Vineyards Pinot Gris 2008 Willamette Valley Oregon USA

This mouthwatering Pinot Gris displays bags of bright fruit, polished winemaking, and great balance. Aromatics range from ripe citrus through to tropical fruits, while in your mouth it's full, plush, and beautifully guided by moderate acidity and a long, fine finish.

This is an excellent example from a benchmark producer and would make perfect company with many Asian salads or a simply grilled salmon steak.

get it from...

$$$$$

www.elkcove.com

Talbott Vineyards Kali Hart Chardonnay 2008 Carmel Valley California USA

Named after Robb Talbott's daughter, Kali Hart is a well-priced Chardonnay made in the lush Talbott style. Trademark tropical fruit character is the main attraction in this medium-bodied, well-balanced bottling. And, while this wine is generally designed for early release and consumption, it's also worth bearing in mind that Monterey County Chardonnay ages very well.

Terrific intensity of fruit, finely knit oak, mineral texture, and superb length suggest we might enjoy this one beyond the prescribed time frame. Fingers crossed.

get it from...

$$$$$

www.talbottvineyards.com

Dr Loosen
Wehlener Sonnenuhr
Riesling Kabinett 2007
Mosel
Germany

The Loosen estate has been family owned and operated for over 200 years, and this wine from the Wehlener Sonnenuhr (the sundial of Wehlen) vineyard is a classic. Planted about 60 years ago, this vineyard produces lovely racy, mineral styles of Riesling that walk the tightrope between sweetness and acidity with ease.

Combining aromas of jasmine, mandarin, spice, and lime, and a racy palate that pulls up just this side of dry, this is a textbook example from one of Germany's top producers.

get it from...

$$$$$

www.drloosen.com

Edmunds St John
Heart of Gold 2008
El Dorado County
California
USA

This is the second vintage of production of this Vermentino and Grenache Blanc blend from California "Rhône Ranger" Steve Edmunds. The grapes, grown in elevated vineyards just above Edmunds' famous Wylie Syrah vines, complement each other beautifully.

The Vermentino provides a lively, spiced component and the Grenache Blanc delivers a floral, perfumed nose and rich, viscous texture. Straw color and a range of pretty aromas lead you to a bright, mineral, and beautifully balanced palate.

get it from...

$$ $$$

www.edmundsstjohn.com

TOP 20 TIPS
#11

Treat your wine with respect

Wine likes to be stored in a cool, dark spot away from vibration, as well as safe from the threat of thirsty housemates.

Penfolds
Koonunga Hill
Shiraz/Cabernet 2008
Multidistrict blend
Australia

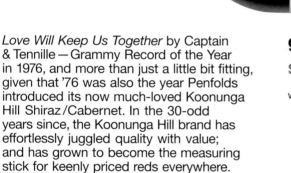

Love Will Keep Us Together by Captain & Tennille — Grammy Record of the Year in 1976, and more than just a little bit fitting, given that '76 was also the year Penfolds introduced its now much-loved Koonunga Hill Shiraz/Cabernet. In the 30-odd years since, the Koonunga Hill brand has effortlessly juggled quality with value; and has grown to become the measuring stick for keenly priced reds everywhere.

A near equal-parts split of Shiraz and Cabernet Sauvignon styled around fruit from the South Australian districts of Barossa, McLaren Vale, and Coonawarra, among others, this wine remains beautifully fruited and sparingly oaked, and a great starting point for what Penfolds do incredibly well.

get it from...

$$$$$$

www.penfoldsvip.com

Wither Hills Sauvignon Blanc 2008 Marlborough New Zealand

Sauvignon Blanc — particularly the Kiwi kind — is perfectly geared toward the flavors of spring, and you would struggle to find a more spring-like dish than spaghetti tossed with the first of the season's fava beans, peas, mint, basil, and a good squeeze of lemon.

Wither Hills produce a cracking example of the Kiwi kind that's both widely available and really good value for money. Pale and pungent, expect plenty of personality with aromas of passion fruit, gooseberry, lime-flavored Popsicles, and soft green herbs, while in your mouth it's intense — packed with all of the above — and beautifully balanced by focused natural acidity.

get it from...

$$$$$

www.lionnathanusa.com

Nepenthe
Adelaide Hills
Sauvignon Blanc 2007
Adelaide Hills
Australia

As great-value examples of Sauvignon Blanc continue to join the endangered species list at an alarming rate of knots, it's nice to know that a couple of Aussie offerings continue to fly the flag for the frugal.

Nepenthe is a much-loved producer from South Australia's Adelaide Hills, and with great-value, cool-climate wines like this, it's not hard to see why. Full of bounce, expect a nose loaded with black currant, spring peas, and soft green herbs, while the palate is fresh as a daisy with bright tropical fruit and mouthwatering acidity.

get it from...

**$$**$$$

www.clickwinegroup.com

Rustenberg Brampton Shiraz 2007 Stellenbosch South Africa

Looking well beyond Chenin Blanc and Pinotage, South Africa's new breed of vignerons are currently putting a number of alternative varieties through their paces. Most exciting in my opinion are the Rhône varietals — and this delicious all-terrain red from the talented Adi Badenhorst is a cracking example of exactly that.

Shiraz is only 90 percent of the story here. Laying the foundation with all that lovely dark-red fruit, chocolate, and spice character, two percent Viognier is co-fermented with the Shiraz to aid texture and aromatic lift, while around eight percent Mourvèdre is blended into the finished wine, adding that ever-so-slightly rustic edge.

get it from...

$$$$$

www.capeclassics.com

Warre's Warrior Port Wine Reserve NV
Douro
Portugal

As the fortified market continues to flounder amid changing tastes and out-of-date marketing, please make a note that this is delicious port for less than $20 a bottle. Maybe one of the best. It also comes with a decent résumé, having been shipped continuously since the 1750s, making Warrior the oldest and most consistent port brand currently doing battle.

Unfiltered and having been matured in oak for an extended period prior to release, this is concentrated and power-packed port with a nose of dried fig, dark plum, and bitter chocolate. In your mouth it's inky and rich, with masses of intensity and a clean, beautifully balanced finish.

get it from...

$$$$$

www.vineyardbrands.com

Beware of gimmicks

The world of wine accessories is full of them, including vacuum-style wine pumps. While sucking excess oxygen out of a bottle, most also have a nasty habit of taking aroma molecules with them, leaving your wine "stripped" of all those lovely smells.

Joel Gott
Zinfandel 2008
Multidistrict blend
California
USA

Coming from a winemaking dynasty — his grandfather was winemaker and president of the historic Inglenook winery in the sixties and seventies — Joel Gott is both well connected and talented. He recently acquired the massive Sutter Home facility in St Helena, from where he vinifies and blends the fruit that he sources from vineyards that fall under the radar throughout the state.

Over the last few years Gott has taken the American Zin market by storm, and this 2008 effort is a classic, with deep, dark cassis, black cherry, and spice. The wine is expressive, well balanced, and shows lovely tannin structure.

get it from...

$$$$$$

www.gottwines.com

Champalou Vouvray Sec Tendre 2008 Loire Valley France

Together, Didier and Catherine Champalou produce some of the finest examples of Chenin Blanc to be found in the Loire Valley. Having established their property in 1984, and covering all bases from fizzy to dry, to oak, to no oak, to sweet, and even sweeter, the Champalous have worked tirelessly to become known as one of the region's true shining lights.

From the dry camp, this is a delicious Vouvray, where a restrained nose of dried apple, honey, and minerals makes way for a palate that manages to be both rich and broad with real weight and intensity, yet without being flabby. Drinking beautifully now, but built to last.

get it from...

$$$$$

www.kermitlynch.com

Donnafugata Anthìlia 2008 Sicily Italy

A surefire contender for feel-good hit of the summer, Anthìlia is a clean and refreshing, equal-parts mix of local Sicilian varieties Ansonica (a.k.a. Inzolia) and Catarratto from Sicilian stars Donnafugata. Production is short and sharp, with fermentation cool and quick, taking place in stainless steel prior to filtering and bottling.

Pale straw to look at, the nose shows plenty of bright, grapefruit-citrus fruit, alongside aromas of green herbs and minerals, and with zero oak influence. The palate is tight, clean, and dry, with stunning intensity of ripe stone fruit— all of which is framed with an acidity so fresh it almost hurts.

get it from...

**$$**$$$

www.foliowine.com

Telmo Rodríguez
Viña 105 2008
Cigales
Spain

High up in Spain's central-northwestern corner, straddling the borders of Ribera del Duero and Rueda, is the increasingly fashionable region of Cigales. Red variety Tempranillo is the local star, producing fresh, fruit-driven wines with bright acidity and dry, grippy tannins.

In the case of this example, great old-vine fruit coupled with the Midas touch of winemaker Telmo Rodríguez— one of my favorite Spanish winemakers— has produced a wine layered with cassis, cherry, smoke, and spice. There is little, if any, evidence of oak, making this a delicious drink-now proposition.

get it from...

$$$$$

www.vintuswines.com

Care about what you drink? Care about what you drink from

Decent glasses needn't cost you a fortune, but they will make a huge difference to the taste of your wine. Store them in a well-ventilated place — not a cardboard box — and hand-wash them in warm, soapy water rather than the dishwasher.

De Bortoli
Gulf Station
Pinot Noir 2008
Yarra Valley
Australia

This is ridiculously cheap and yet phenomenally good Pinot Noir. De Bortoli has really raised the bar with this striking example that effortlessly ticks all the right boxes.

For a start, you get terrific varietal character: sweet cherry, smoke, and spice coupled with a silky mouth-feel and bright acidity. There's even a small lick of nice French oak in there just to really add insult to injury. It's all there, and largely thanks to the men behind the controls, Steve Webber and Bill Downie. A great wine that just goes from strength to strength.

get it from...

**$$**$$$

www.debortoli.com.au

Henschke
Tilly's Vineyard 2008
South Australia
Australia

While it's always lovely to taste the pinnacle of what a producer can do, it's often their cheapest wines that say the most about them. Henschke is a brilliant case in point. At one end of the Henschke spectrum is Hill of Grace—one of Australia's most revered wines—while at the other is Tilly's, a beautifully elegant white that represents seriously good value.

Lovingly assembled from Semillon (57 percent), Sauvignon Blanc (24 percent), and Chardonnay (19 percent), and using fruit drawn from both the Barossa Valley and the Adelaide Hills, expect smells of lemon rind, elderflower, and green herbs, while in the mouth it's vibrant, zippy, and dry. Prior to bottling, the wine spends nine months on lees, giving it great weight and texture, yet the use of oak is kept to a minimum.

get it from...

$$$$$

www.negociantsusa.com

Cono Sur
Visión Merlot 2008
Colchagua Valley
Chile

For many winemakers, Chile's vineyards are the stuff of legend, blessed with a dreamy climate, varied geography, and a seemingly endless supply of water. Just about anything you plant here will grow and prosper, and in the right hands, do so with style — even good old Merlot.

Cono Sur has raised more than just a few eyebrows in recent years with a string of great releases, many from cooler growing zones. From those, this is terrific Merlot, polished and pure with a serious core of dark fruit, chocolate, leather, and spice. The palate is sweet, dense, and inky, with fresh acidity and fine, drying tannin.

get it from...

$$$$$

www.conosur.com

d'Arenberg
The Stump Jump 2007
McLaren Vale
Australia

In the days before fancy diesel-powered farm equipment, the stump jump was an all-terrain plow that had the ability to ride over stumps and tough eucalyptus roots without pause. Today it's more commonly associated with d'Arenberg's much-loved everyday sipper—a wine that ranks as one of the best-value reds from Australia.

Largely assembled using leftovers from higher up the company's vinous pecking order, Stump Jump is an all-terrain blend of unwooded bush vine Grenache, Shiraz, and Mourvèdre. Like others in the d'Arenberg range, production includes fermentation in head-down, open-top fermenters followed by gentle basket-pressing.

get it from...

$$$$$

www.oldbridgecellars.com

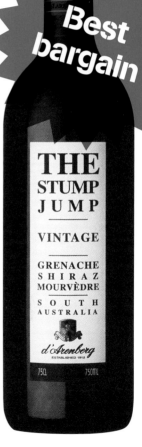

Best bargain

Invest in a decent corkscrew

I know it sounds ridiculous, but it will pay for itself. I have ruined more great bottles of wine than I care to remember by using cheap corkscrews trying to open them. Look for something with an easy action, something that feels strong, and if you can, an opener with a Teflon-coated screw.

Torres
Viña Esmeralda
2008
Penedès
Spain

Viña Esmeralda is a dry and flamboyantly aromatic blend of Moscatel and Gewurztraminer. For a small amount of money you get a huge amount of personality in return.

With zero oak influence, a pretty mixture of jasmine, musk, and litchi are what you can expect to find on the nose, while in your mouth this wine is crisp, nowhere near as rich as you might expect, and beautifully balanced. Besides being radically ahead of its time, today this wine remains one of the best-value whites on the market and a seriously good partner to many examples of Asian cooking.

get it from...

$$$$$

www.dreyfusashby.com

Domaine de Durban Muscat de Beaumes-de-Venise 2007
Southern Rhône France

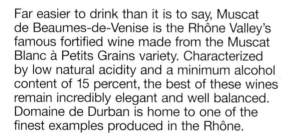

Far easier to drink than it is to say, Muscat de Beaumes-de-Venise is the Rhône Valley's famous fortified wine made from the Muscat Blanc à Petits Grains variety. Characterized by low natural acidity and a minimum alcohol content of 15 percent, the best of these wines remain incredibly elegant and well balanced. Domaine de Durban is home to one of the finest examples produced in the Rhône.

With zero botrytis influence, this is a clean, modern style where aromas of citrus marmalade, apricot, and pineapple dominate. In your mouth expect incredible length of flavor, a little alcoholic heat, and lovely bright acidity.

get it from...

$$$$$

www.kermitlynch.com

Hugel & Fils
Pinot Blanc
Cuvée Les Amours 2006
Alsace
France

Saturday lunch in our house is about recycling. All the leftovers from the last week get a quick spruce before being served on a huge plate in help-yourself fashion. On any given Saturday you'll find some bizarre configuration of olives, caperberries, anchovies, ham, salami, a couple of tomatoes from the garden, chickpeas, avocado, feta, and baba ganoush, always together with plenty of crusty bread.

A couple of glasses of wine and the Saturday papers make it far more civilized, and this perennial favorite from Hugel is bang on the money. Clean and crisp with a nose full of pear, lemon, and honeysuckle character, in your mouth it's soft and delicate with moderate acidity and a long, drying finish — the perfect precursor to a lazy Saturday nap on the couch.

get it from...

$$$$$$

www.frederickwildman.com

Casa Silva Reserva Carmenère 2007 Colchagua Valley Chile

For years Carmenère has been a sore point for winemakers throughout Chile. Getting it physiologically ripe without being overripe is the real key to success, and in this *reserva* Casa Silva do a brilliant job. Its wines always look solid and clean, and here we have something that sings.

Launching straight at you with all the force of a stage dive gone awry, this is a serious attack on the senses. Deep crimson/black in color, the nose is a tightly wound mass of violet, dark chocolate, and sweet, inky fruit. Delicious.

get it from...

$$$$$

www.vindivino.co

Yalumba
Botrytis Viognier 2008
Wrattonbully
Australia

Poached pears with really good ice-cream—
one of those bulletproof desserts made all
the better by a well-chosen wine to match.
But you have to be a little bit careful—you'll
need weight and richness, and nothing too
cloying. Viognier would be a good place to
start. From dry all the way through to sweet,
Yalumba do Viognier better than most, and
this example is no exception.

This is a delicious wine loaded with smells
of grapefruit conserve and sweet tropical
fruits. The palate is plush, sweet, and
characterized by incredible length of flavor
and tight, zippy acidity.

get it from...

$$\$\$$$$\$\$$ (37.5 cl)

www.negociantsusa.com

Sonoma-Cutrer Sonoma Coast Chardonnay 2006
California
USA

It has to be said that there are few places that Chardonnay hasn't sunk its roots. It's been a big winner in the New World, and has developed a real affinity with California's Napa Valley. Unfortunately, a lot of California Chardonnays are overenthusiastically super-sized, with double helpings of oak. Sonoma-Cutrer's Russian River Chardonnay is not one of those.

It's intense and full-fruited, but manages to retain real charm and character at the same time. From its tightly packed, intense nose of grapefruit, cashew, and hazelnut to the finely structured palate, this is a first-class lesson in how good New World Chardonnay can — and should — be. Give it to the doubters.

get it from...

$$$$$

www.sonomacutrer.com

TOP 20 TIPS

#15

Be wary of "special offers"

From experience, "special offers" are rarely all that special. If you really want to find the bargains on the wine store shelf, do a bit of research and seek out the weird and wonderful: new varieties, styles, regions, and countries that you have never heard of. More often than not, that's where the real value lies.

Quinta de la Rosa
Vale da Clara 2007
Douro
Portugal

It's exciting times for Portugal — particularly in the dry red table wine department — and the Bergqvist family's Quinta de la Rosa is certainly one estate worth keeping an eye on. Since 1992 winemaking has been overseen by Jorge Moreira, and from much-loved favorites like this, quality has improved out of sight.

Vale da Clara is an unwooded blend of traditional port varieties, Tourigas Nacional and Franca, and a trio of Tintas, Barroca, Cão, and Roriz. It displays plenty of dark, dried fruit, smoke, and spice on the nose, while in the mouth prepare yourself for fresh and forward fruit, and let bright acidity, cedary oak, and some fine, grippy tannin complete the picture.

get it from...

$$$$$

www.vinumimporting.com

25 wines for indulging

Welcome to the chapter where we throw caution to the wind and bravely show the budget the door. First and foremost know that the wines that appear over the coming pages are not here because of what they cost but rather what they're worth. Know that a huge investment of love, blood, sweat, and tears is more often than not required to produce these wines — some of which are already established benchmarks, while others are modern classics in the making. Finally, remember that with wine you generally get what you pay for, and so in the case of the following 25 bottles, mega attention to detail, microscopic productions, and well-earned reputations count for everything.

Splurge

Brewer-Clifton Mount Carmel Pinot Noir 2007 Santa Rita Hills California USA

Dedicated to creating wines that are true to their terroir, Steve Clifton and Greg Brewer have been making great wines for over a decade. This is the Pinot Noir bottling that best showcases the unique mineral terroir of Mount Carmel. With bright, forward, red berry fruits, an intricate structure unfolds, with silky smooth tannins evident on the finish.

This is an outstanding treat for drinking right now. However, as the elegant structure would indicate, this wine will express even more subtle notes after three to four years in the cellar.

get it from...

$$$$$

www.brewerclifton.com

Paul Hobbs
Cabernet Sauvignon 2006
Napa Valley
California
USA

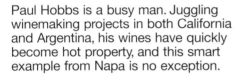

Paul Hobbs is a busy man. Juggling winemaking projects in both California and Argentina, his wines have quickly become hot property, and this smart example from Napa is no exception.

Here, Hobbs manages to bring fruit to the fore with a plush and luxurious example of Cabernet that shows great texture and depth. Solid, cassis-like fruit is nicely framed by a wash of fine, drying tannins on the palate, giving definite notice that, delicious as it is now, this is one for the long haul. Walk over hot coals to get your hands on some!

get it from...

**$$$$**$

www.paulhobbswinery.com

Philip Togni Vineyard Cabernet Sauvignon 2006
Napa Valley
California
USA

It shouldn't come as any great shock that the wines of Philip Togni are more than just a little bit European in their styling. A former pupil of Bordeaux great Emile Peynaud and having served time at Château Lascombes, Togni makes wines with a distinctly European feel that sets them apart from many of the competition.

Black currant fruits and candied anise prevail on the nose, while plush, inky texture and noticeable yet controlled tannins on the palate suggest that this is a wine built for the long term. This is a world-class effort and a dose of fruit purity beyond my wildest imagination.

get it from...

$$$$$

www.philiptognivineyard.com

VILA
VINI
TECA
Emilio Moro
MALLEOLUS SANCHO MARTIN
2003
109,00
VILA
VINI
TECA
PAGO CAPELLANES
EL PICON
1999
RIBERA DEL DUERO
141.00
LOS CAPELLANES
PARCELA
EL PICÓN
Ribera del Duero
Tinto 1999 El Picón
PAGO DE LOS CAPELLANES, S.A.
PRODUCT OF SPAIN
14,5% Vol. 750 ml.e
VILA
VINI
TECA

Anderson's Conn Valley Vineyards Right Bank 2007
St Helena California USA

Todd Anderson has a great reputation for producing Bordeaux-influenced red wines in California. This Right Bank example is similar to a gentle, Merlot-dominated wine from Pomerol. Here, the softer Merlot grapes are blended with about 40 percent Cabernet Franc. This Cabernet Franc juice contributes by providing the wine with a sturdy framework for complexity and aging. Black fruits, rich chocolate, and leather notes dominate, and the wine is truly made to survive the long haul. You could easily lay this one down for drinking 15–20 years from now.

get it from...

$$$$$

www.connvalleyvineyards.com

Domaine Tempier Bandol Rosé 2008
Provence
France

There's only a couple of wines whose impending annual arrival manages to get my heart racing. Tempier Rosé is one of them. Located on France's south coast halfway between Marseille and Toulon and brought to the wine-loving world's attention by ace California wine merchant Kermit Lynch, Tempier is renowned for its five terroir-driven *cuvées* of old-vine Mourvèdre, and for its rosé that boasts a serious cult-like following.

Produced from a mix of Mourvèdre, Grenache, and Cinsault, and with only a tiny amount of time in contact with the skins, the result is a clean, fruit-fresh, dry, and grippy rosé that will have you hooked and on the hunt in no time at all.

get it from...

$$$$$

www.kermitlynch.com

Keep it interesting

It's easy to fall into a wine rut, so make it your business to try new things whenever you get the chance. Sommeliers, wine waiters, and those behind the counter of your local store are not out to get you! Put your faith in them and let them pick something for you.

Ramey Wine Cellars Sonoma Coast Chardonnay 2007
California
USA

This knockout wine from David Ramey is indicative of Chardonnay's new breed. Gone is the heavy-handed use of oak and the everything-but-the-kitchen-sink approach adopted by many. In its place is a wine style that is infinitely more drinkable, more food friendly, and with a greater capacity to age.

Drawn from the cool of the Sonoma Coast, this is a great example where focused and intense citrus fruit provide the foundation upon which you'll find layers of spice, cashew, and mineral. The palate is medium-bodied, finely textured, and long.

get it from...

$$$$$

www.rameywine.com

Robert Sinskey Vineyards Vin Gris of Pinot Noir Los Carneros 2007
Napa Valley
California
USA

These grapes come from Robert Sinskey's Los Carneros vineyards and great care is taken when making this rosé not to over-extract the fruit. The result is an elegant rosé that is soft and pale in color, yet with very robust flavors.

Classic Pinot Noir characteristics are apparent, with spiced red berry fruits and mineral layers aplenty. Extremely well balanced, this rosé shows an enthusiastic, fresh character with a long, lingering finish.

get it from...

$$$$$

www.robertsinskey.com

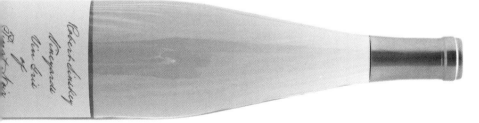

Larmandier-Bernier Terre de Vertus NV Champagne France

The rise of independent Champagne growers such as Larmandier-Bernier, Egly-Ouriet, and Selosse is a breath of fresh air for fizz lovers everywhere. What sets these producers apart from the pack is a determination to capture a sense of place rather than simply to create the usual house style.

Carved from 50-year-old-plus, single-vineyard, biodynamically grown Chardonnay vines, Larmandier-Bernier's Terre de Vertus is a stunning wine with great poise, purity, and balance. Zero *dosage* only adds to the magic.

get it from...

$$$$$

www.louisdressner.com

Phillips Hill
Toulouse Vineyard
Pinot Noir 2007
Anderson Valley
California
USA

This is small-scale production Anderson Valley Pinot Noir, made by the talented Toby Hill. His Toulouse vineyard — which is primarily made up of Pinot Noir from Dijon clones — is ideally located in the Navarro River Fog section of the Anderson Valley. The wine is made true to the traditions and style of Burgundy, with minimal intervention and a hands-off approach to wine-making, which, beyond top-quality fruit, are the keys to success.

Expect smells of wild cherry, raspberry, and sweet spice, while the palate is smooth and complex with nicely knitted oak, fine slinky tannins, and a long, sweet finish.

get it from...

$$$$

www.phillipshillestates.com

Sean Thackrey
Pleiades XVII
California
USA

Named by Sean Thackrey after the Pleiades —
the Seven Sisters — star cluster, this unique
wine is a blend of several grape varietals,
which usually includes: Sangiovese, Syrah,
Petite Sirah, Mourvèdre, Barbera, Carignan,
and Viognier, among others. Thackrey
experiments each year at his property located
one hour north of San Francisco, blending
the fruit to suit his taste. As a result, the exact
percentage makeup varies from year to year,
making it even more interesting.

A red cherry and currant fruit chord usually
prevails, plus a noticeable touch of eucalyptus —
many trees surround his property. So prominent
is this that it has become the signature note
in the blend from one version to the next.

get it from...

$$$$$

www.wine-maker.net

Rediscover your sweet tooth

Don't turn your nose up at sweet wines. Sweet wines rarely get the kudos they deserve and more often than not they will represent some of the greatest value on a wine list. Problem is that by the time we get to them we've usually had enough. Next time, save some room.

Zind-Humbrecht
Zind 2007
Alsace
France

Olivier Humbrecht MW is both a fierce stickler for detail and a true champion of the biodynamic movement. His wines are produced via an enormous amount of effort that includes high-density planting, everything that can be done by hand being done by hand, alcoholic fermentation of all wines in oak, and all vineyard tasks organized and carried out in line with the various phases of the moon.

The attention to detail is as astonishing as the wines. The entry-level Zind is a medium-bodied, off-dry, drink-now blend of Chardonnay and Auxerrois Blanc produced in the house style, and loaded with ripe stone and tropical fruit character.

get it from...

**$$$$**$

www.thesortingtable.com

L Martinelli Martinelli Road Chardonnay 2006 Russian River Valley California USA

I love these complex Russian River Chardonnays and find them impossible to resist. The Martinelli Road vineyard is one of the coolest sites in the valley and is thus ideal for these Dijon-cloned vines to produce their magic.

Made by the talented Bryan Kvamme, with input from renowned consultant winemaker Helen Turley, this Chardonnay displays spiced apple and pear flavors with balanced, crisp, zippy edges and even mineral notes that carry right through to the finish. Neither fined or filtered, nor heat- or cold-stabilized, this is Chardonnay at its purest. To allow any natural sediment to fall to the bottom, you're best to decant this wine, or let it stand upright for an hour before pouring.

get it from...

$$$$$

www.martinelliwinery.com

Hirsch Vineyards The Bohan Dillon Pinot Noir 2008 Sonoma Coast California USA

Stumbling across good-value Pinot Noir is a little bit like finding a needle in a haystack, and so when you do finally come across examples that are not only keenly priced but also well made, it's worth making some noise about them.

From the fabled Bohan Dillon vineyard on the Sonoma Coast, where the North American and Pacific Plates meet along the San Andreas Fault, this tidy example ticks all the right boxes. With plenty going for it, including no shortage of spiced cherry and dark berry fruits on the nose, expect a pure, lively, and well-balanced mouthful of wine that displays plenty of charm and great structure.

get it from...

**$$$**$$

www.hirschvineyards.com

Drink more fortified wine

Port, sherry, liqueur Muscat, and Tokay—these are the endangered species of the wine world. They are also some of the most amazing wines produced in the world, yet because of their higher alcohol content and our taste for drier wines, they are also some of the most unpopular. Please support them before they disappear from our shelves forever.

Domaine la Roubine Côtes du Rhône Gigondas 2007
Southern Rhône France

Taken from an old hillside vineyard near Vacqueyras, this is power-packed Gigondas assembled from Grenache (70 percent), Syrah (20 percent), Cinsault, and Mourvèdre (10 percent between them). Vines here range from 10 to 50 years of age, while the wine is traditionally made, incorporating indigenous yeasts and no fining or filtration.

The results are spellbinding. Expect no shortage of bright raspberry and sour-cherry fruit, alongside smells of trademark Rhône pepper and spice. The palate is plush and well fruited, with mineral intensity and a wash of dry, grippy tannins, some of which come courtesy of well-handled wood — half the wine gets a year in oak, of which only 15 percent is new.

get it from...

$$$$$

www.elitewines.net

Hendry
Blocks 7 & 22
Zinfandel 2007
Napa Valley
California
USA

As Zinfandel goes, this is a hearty example and accurately reflects the fabled Napa terroir from which it comes.

Alongside a plush and richly textured palate, expect smells of sweet, dark fruit, black cherry, and white pepper. Even from first glance this is Zinfandel of roller-coaster-like proportions — from the anticipation that builds as your nose finds the glass, the heady fruit as the glass hits your lips, and then a rush of fruit so intense yet so measured, all of which leads to a long, smooth finish. Who'd have thought wine could be this much fun?

get it from...

$$$$$

www.hendrywines.com

Sánchez Romate Cardenal Cisneros Pedro Ximénez NV
Jerez
Spain

Wow. As a self-confessed sherry freak, I would be the first to admit that I love Pedro Ximénez for its over-the-top, liquid Christmas cake aromatics, for its ripe, velvety mouthfeel, and for its long-as-you-like finish that goes on forever. But this is ridiculous. This takes the experience to a new level.

Take a seat and brace yourself for a nose full of dried-raisin fruit, molasses, Middle Eastern spices, and fresh ground coffee. In the mouth it borders on pouring-cream consistency and comes fully loaded with sweet raisined fruit and cloying intensity. Dried-raisin fruit coupled with aromas of cinnamon, nutmeg, and clove lead to a mouthful of sweet, rich, and cloying fruit, with wave after wave of intensity.

get it from...

$$$$$

www.southernwine.com

Dashe Cellars
Todd Brothers Ranch
Old Vines Zinfandel 2007
Sonoma County
California
USA

Husband and wife team Mike and Anne Todd make a formidable duo. With Mike having once been responsible for Ridge's Lytton Springs winery in Dry Creek, and Anne having studied enology in Bordeaux, the couple married in 1996 and before long Dashe Cellars was born.

The Todd Brothers Ranch comprises 50-year-old vines on a steep, rocky slope just a short distance from Geyserville. The thick, old, gnarly vines produce fruit with sweet raspberry and plummy fruit together with full, inky mouth-feel and a seriously long finish.

get it from...

$$$$$

www.dashecellars.com

Avoid the second-cheapest bottle

The second-cheapest bottle on the wine list is never the best value — every wine buyer on the planet knows that trick. Invest your trust in the sommelier, the wine waiter, or the waiting staff. Give them some parameters on price and style etc., and then let them recommend something for you.

Castellare di Castellina Chianti Classico 2006
Tuscany
Italy

Castellare's beautiful and often underrated Chianti Classico is certainly one of the region's smartest buys. And while many of the area's bigger names become more expensive and more concentrated by the minute, Castellare seems to maintain its cool. Straddling the boundaries between new and old, this stylish and accessible blend of Sangiovese with its splash of local grapes Canaiolo and Colorino, and its annually changing label of treasured but endangered birds, effortlessly ticks all the right boxes.

Right from the word go this is unmistakably upmarket Sangiovese, sporting a nose full of morello cherry, leather, and tobacco, while in your mouth it's plush, mineral-textured, and framed by trademark fine, chalky tannins, finishing clean and dry.

get it from...

$$$$$

www.winebow.com

Pegasus Bay
Sauvignon Blanc/
Semillon 2008
Canterbury
New Zealand

In the beautiful Waipara valley outside Christchurch, the Donaldson family craft some of New Zealand's finest white wines. Besides great examples of Chardonnay and Riesling, they also make one of the slickest blends of Sauvignon Blanc and Semillon I have ever had the good fortune of tasting.

Textured and refined, this is a breathtaking blend where an extended period on lees and the judicious use of oak have paid off big time. Expect a complex nose of white peach, pear, and passion fruit, while broad stone-fruit flavor is carried in the mouth by creamy texture and framed by focused acidity and terrific length. Seamless, long, drinking beautifully now, yet built to last.

get it from...

$$$$$

www.empsonusa.com

Ayala
Brut Nature
Zéro Dosage NV
Champagne
France

The wines of Ayala have improved out of sight ever since Bollinger purchased the property in late 2005. Yet, in stark contrast to Bollinger, Ayala's style relies on being lighter and fresher, making it a brilliant pre-dinner option. The mouthwatering Brut Zéro Dosage — reference to the fact that this wine was bottled without the addition of any sweetened base wine *(dosage)* — is the ultimate apéritif, incorporating a ruthless selection process and utilizing fruit from selected *grand* and *premier cru* vineyards.

With Pinot Noir taking the leading role, expect restrained citrus and stone fruit, toast, and honey. Meanwhile, the palate is full and rich, with plenty of bright bubbles and a long, dry finish.

get it from...

**$$$$**$

www.cognac-one.com

Pol Roger 1999 Champagne France

Having already scooped the prize for the most under-appreciated, non vintage fizz on the market, Pol Roger is set for a repeat performance with its knockout vintage version. Words struggle to describe just how consistently good this wine is, and much like its stablemate, it's simply an essay in both style and value.

Aromas of Pinot Noir fruit and fresh toasted brioche set you up for a mouthful of rich stone and citrus fruit that's creamy and direct, with firm acidity and incredible length of flavor—a genuine jawdropper from one of Champagne's greatest houses.

get it from...

$$$$$

www.frederickwildman.com

Speak up!

If you're not happy with your wine,
tell the sommelier/wine waiter.
That said, you will really only have
grounds to return the wine if it's
corked or oxidized. If you simply
don't like it, chances are you'll be
stuck with it.

Domaine Laroche Chablis 2007 Burgundy France

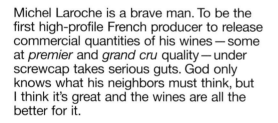

Michel Laroche is a brave man. To be the first high-profile French producer to release commercial quantities of his wines — some at *premier* and *grand cru* quality — under screwcap takes serious guts. God only knows what his neighbors must think, but I think it's great and the wines are all the better for it.

Clean, flinty, citrus, and ever so slightly honeyed on the nose. The palate is delicate and mineral-tipped, with great length and balance. Bravo and *vive la révolution*!

get it from...

$$$$$

www.larochewines.com

Lang & Reed
Cabernet Franc
North Coast 2007
Multidistrict blend
California
USA

Having been subjected to one too many green-edged examples of Cabernet Franc in my time, it's a beautiful thing to stumble across one with such heart-stopping depth and purity.

The brightness and intensity of the top-shelf Napa fruit is here for all to see, married as it is with fruit from the more northerly—and stunning—Lake County. From the intensity of its color to the plushness of its fruit—this is a delicious wine made all the more enjoyable by lively acidity and a stylish framework.

get it from...

$$$$$

www.langandreed.com

Robert Sinskey Vineyards Los Carneros Pinot Noir 2007 Napa Valley California USA

Robert Sinskey's goal is to make "pure wines of character that pair well with cuisine." He believes that wine should not be a "quick study," but rather sneak up on you, seduce you, and evolve in the glass and in the bottle.

His Carneros Pinot Noir reflects this philosophy and also his idea that he is simply a "dirt farmer." Rob farms his Pinot Noir grapes organically and the result is apparent from the monolithic earthy tones present. The fruit purity, finesse, and balance of all suggest that this wine will last in your cellar for many years to come.

get it from...

$$$$$

www.robertsinskey.com

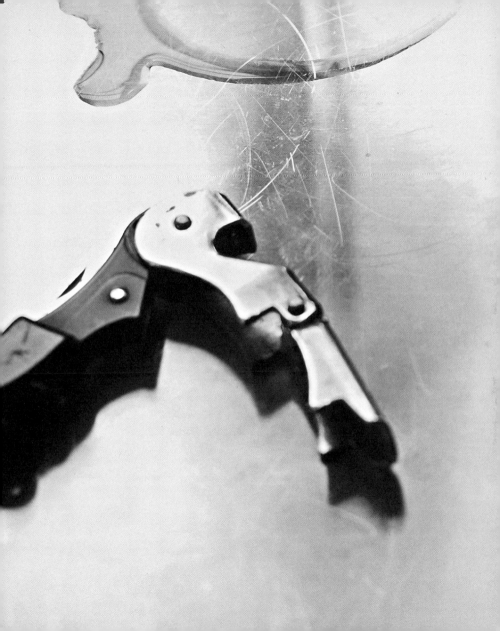

Lustau
Emilín Moscatel
Solera Reserve NV
Jerez
Spain

One of two sweet Moscatels made by Lustau and a step back from the glorious San Emilio PX, Emilín Moscatel is surprisingly light, but still comes packing plenty of personality.

For a start, it's much paler to look at, with a solid, deep copper color extending right toward the outer rim of your glass. The nose is lighter too. Bright and lifted aromas of dried raisins, sweet spice, and oak— of which this wine has seen its share — are all there. The palate is spirity and fresh with plenty of raisiny fruit flavor, yet minus the cloy factor. Be warned: it's a dangerously easy wine to drink and the finish is sweet, oaky, and long.

get it from...

$$$$$

www.europvin.com

Index of producers

Cheers!

The Juice 2010–11 would not have been possible without the help of the following individuals…

Matt Utber, Chris Terry, and all the crew at The Plant and Chris Terry Photography— massive love and respect to you all for once again helping to pull a huge rabbit out of a tiny hat. Also, massive thanks must go to the incredible John Corrigan for helping out hugely on this edition. To Debbie Catchpole and Verity O'Brien at Fresh, and to Lisa Sullivan at Forum 5. Also, big thanks to my right-hand man Chris Franklyn. To all at Mitchell Beazley: Alison Goff, David Lamb, Leanne Bryan, Hilary Lumsden, Becca Spry, Fiona Smith, Pene Parker and Yasia Williams-Leedham. Thanks also to Susanna Forbes. To my extended family: Jamie Oliver Inc and the Fifteen Group (London, Cornwall, Amsterdam, and Melbourne), Jonathan Downey and Match Group (London, Ibiza, New York, Chamonix, and Melbourne), Frank van Haandel, and Roger Fowler. Big shout-outs also to Judy Sarris at *Gourmet Traveller Wine*, Clare Patience at *Home Beautiful*, and Hamish McDougall at *GQ Australia*—thank you all for putting up with my lateness! To those behind the scenes: Mum, Drew, Caroline, Jessie, Eve, Anne, Thommo, Gin, Camilla, Felix, Tobe and George, Randy, Pip, and James, BP, CC, and GG, Jamie and Jools, Ben Gillies and Chris Joannou, David Gleave, Philip Rich, Stuart Gregor, Cam Mackenzie, Andy Frost, The Jones, Cooper-Terry, and Utber clans, Lucas and Indigo at Odo for killer coffee, Dan Holland at Victoria Bitter, The Mighty Hawks, and beautiful Melbourne town.

M x